Community Transformation

A Beginners' Guide

John Leach

Director of Anglican Renewal Ministries

GROVE BOOKS LIMITED
RIDLEY HALL RD CAMBRIDGE CB3 9HU

Contents

The Cover Illustration is by Peter Ashton

First Impression April 2002
ISSN 1470-8531
ISBN 1 85174 496 7

Introduction

1

Since its release in 1999, thousands of British Christians have watched a video called 'Transformations,' along with its 2001 sequel, 'Transformations II—The Glory Spreads.'

These two documentary videos tell the extraordinary stories of different communities in which the renewing power of the Holy Spirit has gone further than just filling individuals, further even than creating 'charismatic' churches, to the point where entire towns, cities and even regions are experiencing renewal. Institutional evil and corruption are being exposed and banished, prisons are closing for lack of any criminals to keep in them, politicians and media figures are finding new life in Jesus Christ and unashamedly going public about it, and even the very land itself is being healed, producing an unprecedented quantity and quality of crops. Communities riddled with substance abuse, domestic violence and hopelessness are finding freedom and prosperity, and of course the Christian churches are experiencing dramatic growth. The videos tell these inspiring stories, and the cry of British Christians goes up 'Why not here?'

In line with Grove's ethos, this is not an attempt to write the last word on Community Transformation ('CT' from now on). I do hope, however, that it might be the first for those many Christians who have not yet seen the videos, or who have seen them and begun to ask about the possibilities at home. My experience after five years of itinerant ministry is that in many towns and cities around England church leaders are experiencing a desire to meet together to pray. I see this as a move of the Holy Spirit, and indeed as a move which is gaining momentum at an accelerating rate. My hope is that this book will help such groups to be aware of what has happened in communities like theirs around the world in answer to that prayer. In particular, I hope it will help to know that there is a well-documented process through which CT has been observed to move, and that this might give some clues to groups of people who have been praying together and have begun to ask the question 'What next?' By identifying which stage in the process you feel you have reached, you may get a clue as to what to do or to expect God to do next. This book, therefore, will be something of a travel guide to lead you step-by-step through the process.

It is worth saying at this point that I believe that CT is what has been called 'the internal logic of renewal.' When I went to work for Anglican Renewal Ministries I inherited a vision statement, part of which said 'We believe that renewal is for the individual, for the church and for the world.' Charismatics majored in the 60s and 70s on getting individuals filled with the Holy Spirit. Later on the emphasis was on creating and running charismatic churches. But many of us were not quite sure what to make of the third area, renewal for the world. While many charismatics were involved in diverse social action and justice projects[1] the movement appeared to lack a coherent strategy for 'renewing the world.' The CT agenda addresses this lack head-on, and provides a paradigm for the logic of charismatic renewal to work itself out fully.

It has been my privilege to attend two major conferences on CT, one in Cape Town and one in Birmingham, to sit at the feet of some of the key players, and to have the kind of job where I have time and space to reflect on some of what God is doing and begin to teach about it around England. I have also had the valuable experience of working in an English city where I believe we saw the very first steps towards CT, even though we did not know at the time that that was what it was called or that anyone was going to make videos about it! My modest aims for this book are fourfold:

- to give a brief account of this move of God;
- to trace what has been discovered about the process of CT;
- to answer some possible objections or hesitations; and
- to list several helpful resources for further study.

I hope you will become excited about the possibilities of CT, and if you are already excited, I hope you will gain some insights which will help you further in knowing exactly what you might do about it.

2

The first person to whom I must introduce you is George Otis Jr, a researcher based with the Sentinel Group in Seattle, Washington State. It is important to understand that George is first and foremost a researcher, and not a theologian—he tells about what he has seen happening, not about what he thinks ought to be happening.

As a researcher he is concerned with the careful collection of data. The videos he has made do set out unashamedly to inspire, but only by recording accurately what is actually going on. This is not about speculative theology or hype! Of course he is selective in what he presents in the videos, and naturally wants to tell us the best stories, but he is very open about the limits of CT (as we shall see later). My point, however, is that this is empirical and not theoretical theology.

Having discovered some communities which had tasted some of the power of God, Otis set out to research them and discover any others like them in order to see if there were any similarities of pattern in what had happened. By 2000 he had fully researched over 40 such places, but was aware of at least as many again which he had simply not had the time to study. At a conference that year he reported:

> Too much is going on. We're talking as fast as we can, taking pictures as fast as we can, but we cannot keep up with the Holy Spirit. Every time we get out to document one or two transformed communities we hear of five new ones. This is utterly unique: it is not the first time revival has broken out, or that a city has been transformed. But what is unique is the magnitude of what is happening in our day.[2]

The Sentinel Group also has on its staff Dr Alastair Petrie, a Scots Anglican minister now working with Otis on researching and studying CT, but with a heart to see it happen within his own Anglican tradition.

Calling All Nations

CT thinking is based around some distinctive theological insights. First of all is the belief that what God really wants is to see nations turning to him, and not just the odd individual convert through local church evangelism. Many biblical texts talk about God's desire to see whole nations coming to him;[3] our vision, say the CT pundits, has simply been too small. Particularly as this relates to charismatic renewal, we have been content to see individuals filled with or baptized in the Spirit, we have tried to build churches where openness to the Spirit and his gifts is *de rigeur*, but seldom have we really expected the Spirit's power to break out in our Town Halls, prisons, schools or businesses. CT thinking reminds us that God's purposes are on a much larger scale than most of us can imagine.

Attracting God's Presence

So why have the places which have experienced some degree of CT done so? Is it the sovereign choice of God, or can we do anything to help it to happen? If it is just God's sovereignty, what makes him choose to move in one place but not in another? The answer is that a community can set out quite deliberately to attract the presence of God. 'What would you get lots of if you wanted to attract Winnie the Pooh to your town?' asks Otis. Answer: 'Hunny.' What about Popeye? Spinach. Or Homer Simpson? Duff beer and doughnuts. So what might attract God to our towns? Unity, says Otis, from Psalm 133, and lots of fervent prayer born out of desperation with the way things are. Again this is not a piece of theology which some may find questionable or facetious; Otis has seen that the places where God has moved are places where Christians have given themselves to fervent, united prayer. So CT is not some random, whimsical act of God—we can deliberately set out to seek it and work and pray for it.

Healing Wounded History

'Spiritual mapping' is another CT principle, not without some degree of controversy. Alastair Petrie has developed a coherent and convincing theology of 'the land,' and he suggests that particular geographical places can become wounded because of events which happened there in the past. In particular three things will lead to this wounding: deliberate false worship (he sees Freemasonry as one of the most significant types of such false worship); bloodshed; and broken covenants or agreements. Such wounded places, if they remain unhealed, will draw evil to themselves as an unhealed wound will, in time, draw flies. 'Spiritual mapping' is simply the attempt through research and discernment to identify such places and to make them particular focus-points for prayer, intercession and/or reconciliation. Some Christians, of course, have used spiritual mapping to identify and then rebuke the 'principalities and powers' which live in and rule over different areas, but this is not a major theme of either Otis or Petrie. The battles need to be fought on the ground through repentance and reconciliation rather than by shouting up into the 'heavenlies.'[4]

Inhibiting Factors

If prayer and unity attract the presence of God, what kind of things might hinder CT, or at least make it particularly necessary? Don Brewin of SOMA[5] expands Otis' thinking about several inhibiting factors, which both have observed in visits to diverse countries experiencing different degrees of oppression. Where any or all of these factors are present (and it is often 'all' rather than 'any') the gospel is considerably less likely to flourish, and Christians will need to research and begin to deal with these issues:

1 Factors to do with past history:

   conflict, racism, injustice, hereditary patterns of illness;

   institutionalized evil, what the Bible calls 'iniquity';

   occult, idolatry, prostitution or other discrimination against or dehumanization of women;

   unresolved sin from the past, which passes down into the next generation in repeated patterns.

2 Inadequate teaching of Christians, particularly about discipleship issues, which leaves them open to influences from cults and other sources.

3 Failure to steward the created world.

4 Immorality, including any situations where Christian leaders fail to set good examples of marriage and family life.

5 Inadequate self-worth, springing from:

   identity confusion (living in a border town: where do I belong?);

   inferiority (Gateshead vs Newcastle, Coventry vs Birmingham);

   living in a 'joke place' (every nation has its equivalent of 'Irish jokes').

6 Broken promises to God, to groups of people, and to individuals.[6]

To overcome these inhibiting factors there needs to be prayer, and lots of it, led by leaders who know how to persevere without getting discouraged, and who are informed by research and mapping. Further, we need to see ever-increasing numbers of Christians who want nothing more than to see God break into their communities join and swell the momentum of prayer.

So how does CT proceed? Once again, is each example a sovereign act of God over which no-one has any control, or is there a pattern, leading to the identification of a specific process which is likely to be repeated more or less predictably? Of course God is sovereign, but Otis, from his extensive re-search, has mapped out a route which he has observed the CT process reliably to follow. From my extremely limited research, I have taken the liberty of adding to it!

The Road to Community Transformation

Otis has documented four distinct stages through which the process of CT passes. Here they are in the form of a large-scale map of the journey; we shall proceed to examine each stage in more detail.

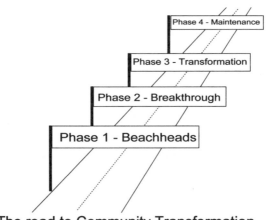

The road to Community Transformation

In expanding and explaining these stages, I have found it helpful to use the image of a road or highway, with what the Americans call 'on ramps' and 'off ramps' ('slip-roads' in English, although for our purposes I find the American terminology more helpful). In other words, during each stage there are things we can do which will feed into the process, keeping us in the right direction and building momentum. But there are also slip roads which we might easily take, with the effect that we move off the main route and get diverted onto side roads.

Phase 1: Taking Beach-heads

3

The image Otis uses is that of a military invasion, where first of all a small area must be secured so that the invading forces can make a base camp from which to continue their assault.

It will usually be small and well-hidden, but it will become a vital first stage for the rest of the journey. This phase is divided into two sub-phases.

1a Fuse-lighting

With a dramatic change of metaphor Otis talks of the need to strike the match which will get the fuse burning, towards the later explosion. What are the on- and off-ramps in this phase?

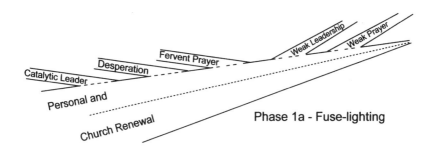

Phase 1a - Fuse-lighting

First of all (and this is one of my additions to Otis' thinking) it is worth noting that the road has come from the direction of personal and church renewal. CT is almost exclusively a Pentecostal/charismatic phenomenon, and those who have closed their own lives to the 'supernatural' power of the Holy Spirit are unlikely to get very far in CT. The prerequisites seem to be a desire for God, a belief in his power to change, heal and deliver as a result of prayer, and a deep fervency and intimacy in prayer. While these characteristics are not, of course, to be found only in those who would call themselves charismatics, they clearly form important values in charismatic spirituality. Other brands of Christians are often drawn in as the process moves further along the road, but they are rarely in at the start of the journey.

Given that background, there is then the need for what I call a 'catalytic leader.' Otis does not mention this, but my own experience and the stories featured on the video have convinced me that moves of God usually begin with a single individual who sees a vision for something better. In the city where I ministered for eight years, an Anglican vicar felt it right to ask God to identify to him other leaders who 'had an anointing for more than just their own churches.' Seven people, myself included, were invited by him to meet regularly to begin praying for the city. Once we were together he ceased to act in any heavy 'leadership' role, but without his initial invitation the group would never have convened itself. Story after story on the two videos show this principle: things begin to happen when one person starts. Some strands of the church would want to call these figures 'apostolic'; I prefer the term 'catalytic' as it avoids interdenominational controversy between different understandings of the role of 'apostles' today.

So first catch your catalyst! As I have taught this material round the country I always ask the people 'Who is the catalytic leader in your town/city?' Sometimes there is clear consensus—everyone knows instantly who has that role (except, sometimes, the catalyst him or herself!). At other times no-one really can say who it is. I then urge them to make that their first and most urgent prayer, that God will raise up or reveal to them the *one* person he is going to use to strike the match which will light the fuse.

Down the next on-ramp comes a real sense of desperation about the state of the community, a holy desperation which comes by revelation from God. It is easy to see how you might be desperate if your community is ruled by drug-barons, or if there is 90% alcoholism, or if the crops are failing, but what of Britain? In a most moving address at the Birmingham CT conference in 2001, John Mulinde from Uganda challenged the Brits, who were saying that we had not seen much CT in our country because we were too comfortable and not desperate enough. He began to open our eyes to the growing secularism, violence, crime, drugs, destructive sexuality and so on in Britain, and his challenge was simple; 'How much worse do you want things to get before you get desperate?' What we need is a *revelation* of how much our nation needs God.

His challenge was simple: 'How much worse do you want things to get before you get desperate?'

Then, in response to this desperation, we need to allow ourselves to be called by our catalytic leaders to fervent and costly prayer. The group of leaders in my city committed ourselves to meetings which began fortnightly and soon became weekly, where we would choose to carve significant times from our busy diaries to cry out to God for the city. Firstly by one man, and soon by a group of seven, the fuse had been lit.

Even at this very early stage, though, we could have lost our way. Two dangerous off-ramps need to be avoided: weak leadership and weak prayer. If there is no catalyst, or if he or she fails to inspire enthusiasm in others, or if the prayer never gets further than 'O Lord please bless Manchester, Amen.' there is little hope of progress.

1b   Building Momentum

The second half of the first stage is about consolidation and momentum-building. After our group of seven had been meeting regularly for a few months we decided that we wanted to spread the net wider. The seven of us (three Anglicans, two Baptists and two New Church) each invited ten people from our congregations to a day when we shared the vision of prayer for the city. It was a significant time, although we had to wait some while before we saw the full significance of it.

It is very easy, after seeing the video clips of all-night prayer gatherings of tens of thousands of people, to believe that the half-dozen in your town praying for a couple of hours a week are not going to achieve very much at all. But Otis reassures us that in virtually every case he has studied the beachhead has been secured initially by a handful of people. Dramatic growth comes later, or at least it does if that initial handful have a desire to draw in others to the task.

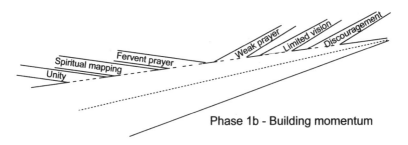

Phase 1b - Building momentum

The first on-ramp in this stage feeds in unity. As our group met to pray it was natural that we began to 'share' (as charismatics call it) more deeply. Several of us turned out to be going through very difficult times, and we prayed for each other as well as for the city. There was some significant reconciliation about inter-denominational hurts from the past—we began to move from being nice to each other to genuinely and deeply loving each other. On one occasion I nearly fell out with one of the New Church people about differing interpretations of the Bible over eschatology, before I caught myself and realized how silly it all was. I was invited to preach in his church shortly after, and I said in my sermon about unity 'What if we do happen to disagree about eschatology? It is not the end of the world!'

Although the seven original members of the praying group were all fully-signed-up charismatics, as we expanded the group others from different strands were drawn in, and this was not always without its pain and difficulties. But we felt the need to hold two things in tension; guarding the vision of praying for our city, and welcoming in all who wanted to be a part of the process. This meant that some of the actual ways we prayed had to be modified: the 'charismatic prayer meeting' approach was enriched as we sometimes celebrated Communion together and used different ways of creative prayer at occasional prayer-concerts.

During this phase Otis mentions spiritual mapping. As we committed ourselves to praying for the city, we felt the need to pray more specifically and deliberately. Through prophetic words and pictures and through some hard work by a Christian archivist we began to explore the wounded past of our city. This in turn fuelled our prayer.

Three off-ramps are dangerous during this stage. Firstly, weak prayer continues to be a danger, but more subtly there can be a real tension between a group of leaders growing deep and open relationships of love and at the same time seeking to expand the group to include others, and indeed even others with a very different style of spirituality. The second danger comes from limited vision, specifically that of seeking unity for its own sake, forgetting that it is unity with a purpose which will keep us moving forward. If we settle down and merely enjoy our new-found depth of relationship with fellow Christians the process will veer off-course into something like a comfortable roadside picnic spot, and the journey will come to a halt. Ruth Ruibal of Cali, Columbia contrasts a 'spirit of unity' with 'unity of spirit' which is an altogether deeper and more purpose-driven level of unity.

'Unity of spirit' is an altogether deeper and more purpose-driven level of unity

The third danger at this stage is discouragement. Prayer is happening regularly, and we really do mean it; God is building deep and genuine relationships. So why is nothing any different? He does not seem to be commanding any blessing around here! Perhaps things have even become worse. In our culture of instant gratification, where we were told that our credit cards took the waiting out of wanting, and where aspirins are sold not on how well they relieve pain but on how quickly, we expect prayer to work in the same way. If our community has not been transformed within six months we will give up and go off on another charismatic fad. Persevering leadership is essential to inspire the discouraged to keep going, and this must be both taught and modelled.

Phase 2: Breakthrough

4

Otis discovered that in communities where fervent united prayer had been sustained there eventually came a stage of breakthrough.

Usually it took years of prayer, often by a small group, and then suddenly there came a sense that things were really shifting. I have moved on and left the city in which I worked and for which I prayed, and I do not think anyone there would yet claim to have seen major breakthrough, although there have been some minor ones. But when it does happen it is unmistakable. There is the sense of being on a roll: there are no off-ramps in this section of the road, because God is powerfully active and it is very easy to go with the flow.

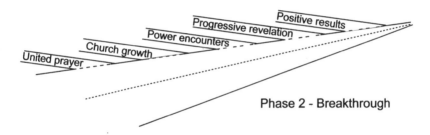

Phase 2 - Breakthrough

There is first of all a dramatic increase in the amount of prayer and of the number of people joining in with it. In the early stages in our city three of the churches agreed that once a month we would cancel our evening services and meet together. The first 'City Celebration' was held in a semi-ruined mediaeval monastic building which some had discerned as a place with residual darkness from the past. About 120 of us met, prayed and worshipped there for about three months, until we outgrew it. Then we moved to my church, which held about 300. When within a few months we grew to over 450 we decided to move again. Finally we filled a city-centre church with over 800, drawn from some 35 different churches. Another highspot was moving to the cathedral, where our Anglican bishop presided at Communion for us. Since I left, the city saw on one occasion over 3000 people crammed into its 2000-seater cathedral. People began to catch the vision. Those ten from each church who had gathered early on in the process began to spread the word, and tens became hundreds.

This is the phase of the all-night prayer gatherings of tens of thousands in football stadiums, as shown on the videos. As the prayer grows, so does the unity between Christians and between Christians and their community. Profound acts of repentance and reconciliation often occur, and groups who for historical reasons have been at enmity find that they can pray and work together again as relationships are healed and the past forgiven.

Dramatic church growth often characterizes this phase: the church begins to have visibility in the community (as 60,000 people in a football stadium all night would!) and non- and de-churched people begin to think again about their faith. This may also be a phase of what John Wimber called 'power-encounters': in some communities where witch-doctors or other occultists have held sway specific prayer sees them exposed and ousted. It remains to be seen what this will mean in the West, where we regard all that sort of thing as just a little bit primitive and superstitious, but I suspect Christians will be in for some surprises when the real powers running our communities are exposed and removed.

The church begins to have visibility as 60,000 people in a football stadium all night would!

Two further things feed momentum into this phase: progressive revelation and positive results. Otis talks about progressive revelation as that quality which keeps you gripped by a good book: the plot is unfolding, the characters are becoming more clearly defined and you simply cannot wait to see what will happen next. You just have to keep on turning the pages. No doubt you are experiencing some of that feeling right now! There can be a sense in this phase of transformation that God is on the move in some ways which are so exciting that you just have to go with it. And of course positive results do have a way of encouraging us. I suspect that one reason why the churches in Britain are so bad at evangelism is that most of them have seldom, if ever, had the privilege of seeing people actually converted. When it does happen it is so exciting that it soon becomes addictive! When people are coming to the Lord daily in significant numbers you do tend to keep praying for more.

You simply cannot wait to see what will happen next

But even with this kind of breakthrough there is still much further to go. The third stage on the journey is the climactic one.

5

Phase 3: Transformation

When the Spirit of God begins to affect society rather than just the church and Christians, the phase of transformation proper has arrived.

The videos document drug-barons being arrested, occultists being driven out, law and order being restored, families being healed, corruption within the council-chamber being exposed, and so on. In one particularly moving story a whole nation, Uganda, is publicly dedicated to Jesus Christ by the President's wife, Janet Museveni, after the horrors of the Idi Amin era. Christians begin to gain significant influence in areas such as education, government, the police force and commerce, even to the point where they outnumber the non-Christians. And God's blessing becomes tangible as prosperity and peace characterize the area.

How do we know we have reached this phase? We read about it in the papers

How do we know when we have reached this phase? Otis is very clear: we read about it in the papers. Communities undergoing transformation grab the attention of the secular media. If Christians are still having to 'talk up' what they think God is doing, they are not yet in transformation. When it arrives the press will beat a pathway to the church door, aware of a profound change in the atmosphere of a community, and feeling something of God's blessing. The reports in the secular media may sound a little mystified, but they will generally be positive.

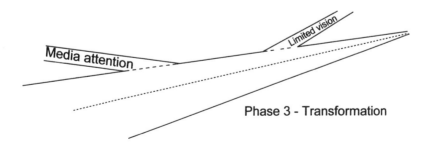

The only real off-ramp during this phase is limited vision which hinders what God is able to do. Any tendency to settle down and see some things as unchangeable 'givens' needs to be avoided so that the prayer becomes more and more specifically targeted and the work of transformation can continue.

Otis has never seen this phase, which is the full bloom of CT, last for more than a maximum of three years, although as CT becomes more and more a feature on the spiritual landscape, who knows what might happen? But even if it is currently time-limited, the Transformation phase is very exciting to live through.

Phase 4: Maintenance

6

The CT journey must move on from Transformation into the next phase.

The word 'maintenance' is a boo-word in contemporary church circles, often used to speak of something which is the very opposite of mission and growth. However, Otis uses the word differently, in the sense of gathering in the fruits which come after the blossom of transformation, rather than leaving them to wither and die, so that everything returns to the way it was before. It is not a static word; it speaks of keeping the momentum going. I may acquire a new car; the task is then for me to see that it is maintained so that it keeps running, not that it sits by the kerbside and rusts.

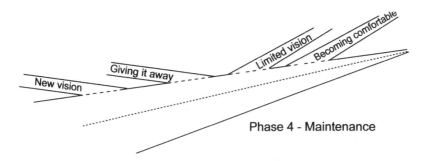

There is the need, therefore, to keep momentum flowing down the on-ramps. Two things are important. The first is to grasp an ever-larger vision of what God might want to accomplish. The first *Transformations* video tells the story of four towns or cities; the second, subtitled *The Glory Spreads*, tells of whole regions being transformed, and even a whole African nation. Just as the church was becalmed for many decades because its vision for renewal spread little further than the creation of a few megachurches, so CT can be self-limiting unless we seek even greater visions to pray into reality. I hope that those who still live, work and pray in my ex-city will see breakthrough and transformation, and if they do I hope that they will then go on to pray for the transformation of the Midlands, then England, then Europe. A limited vision can provide an effective off-ramp which will divert and dissipate the energy for transformation.

Becoming comfortable is another danger. To live in a place where 90% of the population are committed, Spirit-filled Christians, where there is negligible crime or violence, where peace and prosperity characterize the atmosphere, and where the next generation of children are being trained and educated into godliness must be a wonderful thing, but one can easily see the temptation to settle down, praise God for what he has done, and take life easy. The one lost sheep is forgotten in the rejoicing over the 99, as are the wayward sheep of the next-door farm.

So what might counter this dangerous tendency towards comfort? Here I turn to an insight not from Otis (although I am sure he would not disagree with it) but from John Wimber. He taught and modelled continually the principle that if you want to increase in knowledge, power *Stored-up knowledge* and anointing you have to give away what you have al*or resources, like the* ready got. He would frequently tell audiences on his min*manna in the desert,* istry trips that the material he was teaching was only this week's; it was provisional, they were learning more all *crumble away if we* the time, but they were willing to share where they had *hold onto them* got to so far. Many times in parish ministry I have found this principle to be a sound one, whether in terms of finance, expertise or personnel: what God gives us he gives us to give away. Stored-up knowledge or resources, like the manna in the desert, crumble away if we hold onto them.

So this same principle ought surely to apply to CT, and in fact is being worked out practically. There is apparently a group meeting regularly in Cali, Columbia, one of the cities featured in the first video, to pray specifically for the UK and its transformation, while some of the city's leaders have travelled to Britain to teach on CT principles. Missionaries from some parts of Africa are moving to darkest England to preach and teach the gospel. SOMA Uganda has recently been started, the first SOMA to be set up in what had in the past been a 'receiving' country. Where God has blessed a nation, the onus is on that nation to become a blessing to others—that was meant to be the function of Israel, God's chosen people in the Old Testament. Transformed communities have a duty to seek the further transformation of others.

Asking Some Hard Questions 7

Has Anything Really Changed in Some of the Places Featured in the Videos?

The danger of videos which quite deliberately set out to inspire Christians, expand their vision and enthuse them about prayer, is that they can appear over-triumphalistic. The first video, for example, tells the story of Cali, Columbia, a city ruled by drug-barons who held the government and judiciary in their grip. Following prayer the criminals' power was removed, the police force cleaned up, and significant CT had clearly taken place. The cost of this was the death by shooting of the man who was the 'catalytic leader' in that community. What the video does not tell us is that the man who shot him is still alive, free, and living next door to his widow, who cannot leave the house without an armed guard. Similarly Uganda, officially rededicated to Jesus Christ, is still listed by the UN as one of the most corrupt nations on earth. Kiambu, a town featured in the first video, was visited by a SOMA team in late 2001, who found a spiritual atmosphere which was still very dark. Transformation, however clearly it has begun, has not been total and complete.

Transformed communities are not perfect communities and still have a long way to go

But how realistic is it to expect that it could be? Otis is clear that transformed communities are not perfect communities and still have a long way to go. We should not compare them with some vision of perfection which is not in any case attainable this side of heaven; rather we should compare them as they are now with the way they were years ago before God moved. And of course we know that the effects of a move of God are not always seen instantly; the changes which resulted from the ministry of the Wesleys in Britain, for example, took about 50 years to work themselves out. This is not always clear from the videos, which quite understandably set out to paint a positive picture of God's work, and which can easily telescope events into a much shorter timescale than they actually took in real time. We do not, after all, need documentaries to tell us that the world is not perfect, or that things move slowly. We only have to look around to see that.

Is This Just 'Prosperity Gospel' in a Different Guise?

No, I do not think it is, for two reasons. The first is that in most of the communities documented so far there is a move of God which begins among the poor, oppressed and marginalized, whereas much Prosperity teaching seems to come most often from among white, well-off capitalists, and to teach them how to become better capitalists.[7] Secondly, though, it seems to me that one major area in which Prosperity teachers have got it wrong is the confusion of individual prosperity, which I am not convinced the Bible teaches us to expect, with community or national prosperity, which it very clearly does.[8] In other words, if I do the right things I have no guarantee that my life will get any better (in fact it may well get worse), whereas a nation which embraces God's ways has biblical promises that it will prosper. Of course individual prosperity may well follow from community prosperity, but the reverse is certainly not true. And in any case the 'Wimber principle' still applies: what God gives us he gives us to give away.

So I believe that there are some considerable differences between what we are seeing in CT and what the Prosperity teachers promise us on their TV shows.

Why Are Most of the Transformed Communities Featured in the Videos from the Developing World? Why Is It Not Happening in the West?

A good question! I have already mentioned the general lack of desperation in the Western church. It is not that there is nothing about which to get desperate, but rather that we are numbed into complacency by the comforts of our consumerist lifestyle. I was brought up sharp by an African speaker at a CT conference who told the story of a weekend he was running for another church where things were not going well—he just was not connecting. So he went home on the Saturday evening to pray, and spent all night on his face before God. Finally, at 6am, God spoke to him, gave him a word for the Sunday morning, which he then just had time to write up before the service began. Of course, the effects of his sermon were immediate and dramatic. Major breakthrough was achieved in that church.

Most Western Christianity stands guilty as accused by Christians from the developing world as being flabby and ineffectual

I could not help but reflect on similar experiences in my life. I too have known that despair point on Saturday evening when I have felt that nothing had got through, and that I was wasting everyone's time. But rather than staying up praying all night I would go home, pour myself a drink and watch *Casualty*! Most Western Christianity stands guilty as accused by Christians from the developing world as being flabby and ineffectual.

However, it is a mistake to believe that such CT is completely absent from our own nation. We may be several stages back from complete transformation, but a momentum is growing, and there are already small signs of hope. For a while in my city there was specific, targeted prayer about the crime rate, which resulted in a measurable drop in the statistics, and this was reported in the local press. A similar thing apparently happened during Message 2000 when Manchester was invaded by Soul Survivor. We have yet to see significant breakthrough or full-blown transformation in contemporary Britain, but that is not to say that God is not on the move, or that there have not been small victories. And there are tremendously encouraging signs that ever-growing numbers of people are hearing and obeying God's call to fervent, united intercession. All around the country groups are meeting to cry out to God for their communities, and one thing is sure: when God calls people to prayer it is because he intends to answer it!

How is CT Different from Revival?

In the late nineties there was fervent hope in Britain (and indeed not a few prophesies and promises) of impending revival. Christians devoured books with accounts of past revivals, and explored different keys which were supposed to bring it. Toronto and Pensacola were both held up as models, and excitement was in the air. But as the millennium came and went and revival still tarried, the mood changed to one of disappointment. Special meetings were discontinued, and some at least of our church life returned to normal. Is the current furore about CT nothing more than a resurrected hope of imminent revival?

Community Transformation is about something much more far-reaching and subtly more world-affirming

George Otis has said publicly that he believes that this move of God in CT is the big final push which will herald the return of Jesus; others are perhaps more cautious. But several factors suggest that revival and CT are not exactly coterminous. Although the word is often used loosely and with several different nuances, 'revival' popularly refers to God waking up his church, calling sinners to salvation and growing the Christian community significantly. CT, however, refers to something much more far-reaching, and subtly more world-affirming. Revival is about what God wants to do with his church; CT is about what he wants to do with his world, including the very created order itself. In that sense revival may be said to be a desire born out of an Enlightenment view of 'man as the measure of all things'; what *really* matters is that lots of individual people find salvation in Christ. CT, however, is much more holistic (and indeed more biblical) in its hope of the redemption of communities and even creation itself being renewed, of the poor finding justice and the broken healing.

Of course revival may be (and often has been) the first step in transformation; the changes in British society which followed the Wesleyan preaching of the gospel are well-documented, for example. But revival need not proceed to transformation, and there are examples of a move of God which has brought many into the church but left the world around relatively unscathed. It is ultimately about vision; God is so often limited in what he chooses to do by what we expect him to do, believe he can do, and cry out to him to do. So revival is a good place to begin, but it needs to go much wider than the church, and more deeply into the very fabric of society.

8

Conclusion

There is much about the whole subject of CT which commends itself as an exciting move of the Spirit of God.

Indeed, many Christians seem instinctively and spontaneously to have gained something of a vision for the healing of their towns and cities, and have begun to meet with other like-minded people for prayer. My hope is that this book will help such people become better informed as they draw on the experience and expertise of those who have seen CT in action in some quite dramatic ways, and also stimulate some who have not yet sensed God's call to begin deliberate, sacrificial united prayer with others in their locality. At a time when many are saying that charismatic renewal has run out of steam, to grasp the opportunities presented by CT seems to me a significant way of allowing renewal to work out its logical conclusion, as we pray fervently that by his Spirit God will fill individuals, renew churches, and also transform whole nations.

If you have not yet seen them you need to begin with the videos. *Transformations* and *Transformations II: The Glory Spreads* are both available from:

Gateway Christian Media Ltd
PO Box 11905
London NW10 4ZQ
0870 011 8184
orders@uksentinel.com

Audio tape sets are also available from two British conferences held in 2001, in Birmingham and Cardiff, from the same address. Key books include:

George Otis, *Informed Intercession* (Regal, 1999)
This is the basic book by Otis on the principles which I have tried to summarize in this introduction to CT, and should be the first port of call for any wishing to read further and expand my noddy guide.

If you do not like reading, the material is available as an audio-taped seminar called *Unleashing the Power of Informed Intercession*.

George Otis, *The Twilight Labyrinth* (Chosen Books, 1997)
In this book and audio-tape set Otis explores some of the reasons why some areas seem spiritually darker than others, and what prayer and mapping can do about it.

There is also a tape and/or video set by George Otis called *Establishing Beachheads* which sets out the first steps in the CT process.

Alastair Petrie, *Releasing Heaven on Earth* (Chosen Books, 2000)
As mentioned, this book sets out a biblical theology of 'the land' and its spiritual significance, including the ways in which places can become wounded.

Russ Parker, *Healing Wounded History* (DLT, 2001)
Russ Parker shares some of his practical insights on dealing with the past sin and hurts which can affect the current spiritual climate of different areas.

In addition other well-known books have a bearing on the subject of CT:

E Silvoso, *That None Should Perish* (Regal, 1994)
J Dawson, *Taking our Cities for God* (Charisma House, 2001)
C Peter Wagner, *Breaking Strongholds in your City* (Regal, 1993)

All these resources are available from Gateway at the address above. They also produce a catalogue with many more CT resources.

The main Sentinel Group website address is: www.sentinelgroup.org

Two SOMA training manuals *Healing of Community Memories* and the more substantial *Renewal for Life* are available from:

SOMA UK, PO Box 6002, Heath and Reach, Beds, LU7 0ZA
01525-237953
SOMAUK@compuserve.com

Notes

1   See Nigel Scotland, *Charismatics and the New Millennium* (Guildford: Eagle, 2000) p 317ff for details of some such projects.
2   From the Transformed Communities Consultation, Cape Town, November 2000. Quoted in my 'Soma without Snakes' *Anglicans for Renewal* 85 (2001) p 7.
3   See for example, among many such verses, Ps 2.8, 22.27f, 46.10, Is 2.2, 5.26, 11.10 and Rev 15.4 and 21.24f.
4   Alastair Petrie, *Releasing Heaven on Earth* (Grand Rapids, MI: Chosen Books, 2000). See also Russ Parker, *Healing Wounded History* (London: DLT, 2001).
5   SOMA stands for 'Sharing of Ministries Abroad,' a charismatic Anglican agency which does short-term missions, particularly to developing countries.
6   These areas are covered in more detail in the SOMA Training manuals *Healing of Community Memories* and *Renewal for Life*. See the resources section above for further details.
7   This is no doubt a crass generalization, but I see little evidence of the embracing of Prosperity teaching by those who humanly speaking ought to need it most!
8   Space prevents my expanding on this, but briefly the OT (and particularly the Deuteronomic strand and the Wisdom literature) work from the basis that both communities and individuals will prosper if they remain faithful to God. However, this view is modified in later strands with regard to individuals; Psalm 10 asks why wicked people still prosper, Job asks why good people fail to prosper, and Ecclesiastes notes that even prosperity might not be the be-all-and-end-all. The NT calls individual followers of Jesus to suffering and sacrifice rather than to prosperity, but nowhere does the Bible question or deny the understanding that corporate prosperity provides a sign of God's favour. Whilst prosperity is a sign of God's blessing, its absence is not always a sign of his displeasure.